OH IF YOU
WOULD ONLY LISTEN

OH IF YOU WOULD ONLY LISTEN

You just might learn something

LAURA FEISE-DORK

iUniverse, Inc.
Bloomington

Oh If You Would Only Listen
You just might learn something

iUniverse books may be ordered through booksellers or by contacting:

iUniverse
1663 Liberty Drive
Bloomington, IN 47403
www.iuniverse.com
1-800-Authors (1-800-288-4677)

ISBN: 978-1-4620-5226-4 (sc)
ISBN: 978-1-4620-5227-1 (ebk)

Printed in the United States of America

iUniverse rev. date: 10/13/2011

My original idea for writing this book was to help as many teenagers as I could through their rough years. First of all, believe it or not I too was a teenager once. I have raised many of my own and a few that were not. I am a Great-Great Grandmother to many teenagers, a Great-Grandmother to even more and a Grandmother to many, many more. I have learned plenty from this wonderful family I have been blessed with. Some teens learn faster and therefore think they are smarter but their brain still has to grow. We learn as we grow. But let me tell you teenagers something. The way to learn faster is to listen to someone who has been through some hard times and good times and has a good understanding of the consequences of our actions. I love writing about young people and I think most adults would agree that teenagers think they know it all. Well, you don't. Think about it. When we first came into this world we were helpless. We could not feed ourselves or take care of anything on our own. All we could do was eat and fill our diaper, this came naturally. We were all born the same in that regard. Then, as we grew, we started to learn; each according to our culture, our race and our religion, forming our own opinions and attitudes. All I'm trying to say is, think about it teenagers. Your parents helped you get to where you are, they taught you to eat, to walk, to talk and yes, they even taught you how to go to the bathroom. Now many of you actually think you are smarter than your parents? Give me a break. Just give them a chance to help you. You think you know it all? Sorry honey, you don't.

I'm not an authority but I would consider teenagers to be definitely the most complicated and misunderstood people I know. You can bet I have learned and am continuing to learn plenty from this group. Teenagers usually share some of the same problems no matter what but oh how different things are today. These days there are so many children getting too much too soon. Too many toys and too much worldly experience have turned too many beautiful young children into greedy, ungrateful, disrespectful little brats. Books, movies, television and the Internet have caused some to think sex with anyone at any time is acceptable. It is so refreshing to actually find some that believe that sex is something special and they are willing to wait for it. Anticipation is just as important.

There are so many new things children can have without earning anything. Some feel everything that belongs to their parents belongs to them, even when they leave home! Sorry honey now is the time for you to earn your own way. It's so hard to convince young people how important they are. They are our future. What fun this book has been for me. I have so many young people entering my life every day. I get to see and hear so many different minds working. I still say children of today are pretty much the same; all trying to get what they want in life right away but it's most always too much too soon. Oh what I learned through my family and friends as I grew. Fortunately, I'm happy most of the time.

I asked, "What if I cannot tell if they are doing something wrong?" "You'll know," was all she said. Believe me I knew. There are so many new things a young teenager has to face today. I hate to admit it but I probably would not have taken care of my Grandma if it was up to me, hey I was only thirteen. I was a real tomboy. I loved playing marbles and climbing trees. This alone should show you how young in mind I was. The railroad tracks were near our home and my brothers and I climbed on boxcars. I just was going to have fun; that is, as a child's thoughts of fun. But when Grandpa died and Grandma came to live with us I was assigned to take care of Grandma. That's a weighty responsibility for a thirteen year old but I was so shy and compassionate I guess my Mom just knew I would not only do it without question but I would do it with love. My sister Betty was fifteen so you would think she would have been elected to that position but there was no way she would take care of Grandma. I was next in line. Of course I would. I did not realize it at the time but I truly was fortunate to be given this opportunity to learn so much from her. God knew what was in my future. I really was not happy at first; she could not do anything for herself. Strange as it sounds though, the more I did for her the more I loved her. This was where I learned to love reading. Each night I took a book, first it was the Bible. I never understood half of what I was reading but Grandma would explain as I read. I loved reading all of her favorite books. This gave her happiness. She had so little happiness. Her eyesight was poor along with everything else that was wrong with her. She gave me so much wisdom. I wish my Grandma would have been able to write about her feelings. That is one of the reasons I feel so strong about writing about mine; how I feel and what I have learned. I want my grand kids to know all about me. I wish my kids would have known her. She taught me plenty. This was one of the reasons I thought I was grown up. To be grown up, well it takes on a different meaning as we grow. Some thirteen year olds today act much older but their minds are not developed. They are still only thirteen. A few of my granddaughters and great-granddaughters have already witnessed one or more births of their own family. I can't even imagine being that age and watching my mother or my sister or my aunt give birth. It just wasn't done. At thirteen I still thought babies came in the black bag the doctor brought to our house. I'll admit that most kids even back then were not as green as I was but never the less I still contend that children know and see more today than children should. They are told so much more than I was. This is good in a way, in that it makes them a little less green and a bit more prepared. But it also tends to make them think they are so smart and are ready to go out on their own. The parents even start thinking that too. Help a child develop wisely by controlling their intake, if you can, of harmful information. Or maybe it's not just the harmful information. Maybe it is just too mature for their little minds to fully comprehend. All the wrong ideas they take in will hurt their minds and bodies. It should start when they learn to walk, right along with their ABC's, which we learn by rote and they stay with us all our life. If they are taught about the harmful effects of smoking, drugs, pre-martial sex and the use of bad language, this would help them in their teens. It certainly helped me. Grandma scared the heck out of me regarding all the above mentioned. When I was confronted with the smoking and drinking that my friends were doing I did not think twice about refusing. In fact they used to call me Baby but I was undeterred. We need to teach our children to take care of themselves at the beginning of life. Sounds funny of money, I had very little. We both had problems. Love, real love, is so important.

Raising children helps a woman to grow. Just because you have a baby does not make you a good parent. You have to learn how to be a good parent. You learn along with your child, as I did. Young or old, our minds go wild pondering on all that lies ahead. Just look at your life behind you ten years ago. Things change so quickly. Realize how much you've learned and know that you will learn so much more. We never know it all.

Sometimes we feel that just because our children are teens or young adults we assume they should know better or have more respect. That is something that children need to learn very young, by listening to and observing the actions of their parents and other family members and friends. That is why it is critical to watch what you say and do and be mindful of the actions of the people you allow your children to associate with.

This is something that I need to tell young people. First your parents are your "boss". When you go out to work, you get another boss. If your parents tell you to do something and you don't, hopefully they will give you consequences to deal with. Otherwise you will find out the hard way later. When your work boss tells you to do something, and you don't, the consequences could be dire; you could find yourself being shown your way to the door. More parents should show their grown children the way to the door if they are not participating fairly by the house rules. It helps prepare them for the reality of life after leaving home. Your parents are paying for everything and they only want the best for you. It's their job to guide you in the right direction. So if you live under their roof, they should be in charge until you go it alone and pay your own way. Now you can live your own private life. Young people think they should have rights to make their own rules when they are growing up and under their parent's roof.

It's time to go back again to the old school. I knew my parents were in charge. I respected their wishes. It is getting worse today. Each young person thinks they are grown up while they are still at home. That's fine if they are acting like an adult, sharing in all the responsibilities and obeying the house rules as set in place by the homeowner. Unfortunately young people often think they can do anything they want. Oh they think they know so much more about everything. But then again their minds are too young to go it alone. They think their parents should stay out of their private life. HEY, you want a private life; go get one on your own. Actually I think it is good to give everyone in the household a certain amount of privacy but sometimes this needs to be earned. If a parent becomes suspicious of or concerned about their child or young adult's behavior all bets are off if you are still living under their roof. They have the right to come into your room for inspection just as a boss sets the rules for your work area. Believe me it is for your own good. If you learn this at home you will not have to suffer the humiliation of maybe being called on the carpet or maybe even being fired from your job. All because you thought you could make the rules to fit you. You will enjoy your life later if you happily let your parents help you along the way. Be grateful they care enough to want to teach you what is right. There are so many older people with so much time invested in life's lessons that are willing to give it to you for free. Take it. But be careful. There are also many people that are willing to give you a lot of useless and wayward information. Don't take it. Get hooked on the stuff that is good and worth learning. There are many older people having trouble now because their teen life is coming back to haunt them.

Something that really bothers me is when I see a young person being given the privilege to drive before they are actually ready. I don't think just having a license means that you are necessarily ready. If you don't have the required and basic respect for the moving tank you are maneuvering down the road or the people you are sharing the road with, you have no business driving. I have seen so many people driving carelessly and recklessly with a "look out for me and get out of my way" attitude. They really think they are the only ones on the road and if something goes wrong it is always someone else's fault. I live close to a high school, believe me I have seen plenty. Talking or texting on the phone and driving is against law people! Yet many people, not just kids, still do it. I've watched some people stopped at a red light that were talking or texting and suddenly just started going right through the light when they thought it had changed. Once again the saying applies; too much, too soon. Too much texting while driving can make you jump the light too soon. I think they call it over stimulation these days. I just call it "wake up dummy." It also irritates me when parents just buy their kids a car without even having them share in the cost. This does not contribute to the respect for the car or a healthy attitude towards learning to earn. Working helps a kid grow up but it should be appropriate to the age. I was working way to young for what was expected of me. As it turns out though, it didn't hurt me one bit. If you learn to work for things you need and want what a better life you will have.

I could tell you plenty about how teenagers think just by watching and listening to them. Each one has a different mind of what they plan to do with their new life ahead yet it's all pretty much the same. Some have a plan, others think they can just wing it and off into the wild blue yonder they go. Some actually watch their feet while others just plod head-on into every mud puddle and pothole in sight, learning the hard way. I am so happy there are programs out there that will help young people find themselves. I am so happy when some actually pay attention and learn that keeping their nose to the grindstone doesn't just wear the skin off their nose but it can assist them with having a good life and still have time left over for fun. Hey, I understand how it feels to want to have a good time. I still like having a good time. I also understand that my idea and their idea of a good time may differ but sometimes it can be the same. Teenage time is one of the most confused times in your life. You just stepped out of being a child. Your parents have always told you what to do or someone is in charge of you. Between the age of thirteen and nineteen your brain explodes. Now you think you know just what is good for you? Sorry honey, you have only just begun to learn. Believe me, I have been there and done that. Oh how smart I thought I was at nineteen. Off into the world I went. I was going to show my parents just how capable I was. First, going out on my own was not easy for me because I truly never had a chance to grow up. I stayed a little girl for so long. I never had friends my age. I didn't know how green I was, but Grandma knew. I knew absolutely nothing that was going on in the world. Oh I knew about the World War that was going on and how hard it was to make a living. But in my personal life, I was still a child at nineteen. And here I was thinking I was ready to be an adult and take care of myself. After all, I had been working out in the world since I was eight. All I can say now is WOW, how I thought I was ready. I was just anxious to be on my own. When I got my first job oh how grown up I thought I was. Most nineteen year olds these days truly are ready but most have not been as sheltered as I was. A funny thing happened when I applied for my first job, the boss of the company actually thought I was thirteen! I had to go home and get my birth certificate to prove my age. This should show you how young I looked and acted. You bet I had determination though. That was my saving grace. My mother had always taught me to hold my head up high. Young people of today are told so much more about life but their brains are still the same; young and underdeveloped. So here I went out into the wild blue yonder, feeling pretty good about my newly found freedom. I got that job in the curler factory and I was so proud of myself. That was my first job outside my home where I had control over all the money I made. I found a home that not only rented me a room but there was one meal a day included and I was able to wash my clothes there too. The rent was a mere $3 a week. Boy did I have it made. My wages were $53 every two weeks which was given to me in cash. There was no income tax then. Now was the time I had to learn how to manage my money all on my own. Working and managing your own money is one of the primary beginnings of growing up. Your mind is not ready but this is when we really start to learn. That's the way it was for me anyway. If only I would have kept growing and learning on my own but no, I automatically thought the next step was marriage and it was on my mind. I met this handsome man that worked right along side of me and he swept me off my feet. Oh how I wanted to be a wife, have a home of my own and little children running around. So, against my parents' wishes, we married. I remember thinking, "What business is it of theirs? Who did they think they were?" Those were some famous last words. I was in listened. What she learned in such a short time. There were about six girls telling their stories of their wrong turns.

I finally got to go to college at fifty-seven. This helped me to get a job working with teens that were going the wrong way. I worked in a group home and was assigned to six teenage troubled girls. Believe me they thought they knew it all, until they were stopped. Some grew up fast, some took a while longer. Even living in a group home some of these darling girls knew just what they could get away with. One ran away and one got pregnant. One of them got a job babysitting. The parents of the kids she was caring for actually let her smoke marijuana. She actually thought she could come back stoned and I wouldn't notice. Even if it wasn't for the pungent odor or the red eyes, I could always tell when one of them was lying by their actions. I was given that gift from raising so many children. Nine times out of ten I could tell when any of my kids were lying. I enjoyed this job very much. Everything came second nature to me. I taught so many things; how to care for your children, how to find and keep a job, the importance of being honest.

We had a group meeting every night after dinner. I liked sitting on the floor in a circle so I could face each one and oh what I learned from these beautiful girls. I was happy I had the opportunity to assist them with ways they could accomplish the hopes and dreams they shared. When you are a teenager you think you know it all. I have enjoyed listening to all the teenagers in my life tell me how much they have learned in their teen years. Believe me I had more fun in life after I grew up. Now I get to watch my grand and great grandchildren grow. It makes me so happy when some listen. When I see some going the wrong way most of the time all I can do is shake my head and know that they are going to learn the hard way. Sometimes it's not really bad,

Like I always say your brain can make you happy or sad. Some people need help with adjusting their thoughts. Our brains are on the job day and night. There's good and bad, it is up to us to flush out the bad. This is the problem we are having with people, troubled minds.

Some people you can help a little but they still carry so many burdens in their mind. We hold so much inside. Only the Lord knows your inner thoughts. There are so many "self" people in this old world, too bad. Oh how things would be different if we would listen to the Lord and his teachings and love those around us. We are not the only person on this earth. Give and take, give plenty and take little. Too many people want everything their way. Look how money talks. We are all important to the Lord. Your money does not help unless you do something good with it. Money can buy you plenty of fun and maybe get you that beautiful person you want in your life. But money can ruin a marriage, too much or not enough, either way. Oh we need money to live. I am happy with what I have. Looking back is our teacher, our hindsight.

Teenage time, now is the time we need excitement, we can handle anything. Some say, "I can do whatever I want; smoke, drink, try a little pot, do a few drugs. I won't get hooked I just want to try it. After all, I am in charge of my own life now. All kinds of people do it, kids, and adults, how bad can it be?" The young people that I went out with drank and told dirty stories. They always had to have a bad word in their conversation. They smoked too. It was hard for me to handle. I did not know about life. Oh I knew how to work but there was so much more but of course I did not realize it. To tell you the truth they frightened me because Grandma put so much fear in me. I watched them misbehave so much. Truly they puzzled me. Because I would not do what they were doing they called me Baby. I soon discovered just what a sheltered life I had been living. I did not care, my sheltered life kept me safe. I turned to the Lord so much then. My Grandma helped me to understand how I could get help with the Lord when I needed it. You can bet I needed it then. I wanted to belong but I was still full of fear. This is the problem with all the young people. All I'm saying is do not fall into that trap. They call it peer pressure today. Take charge of yourself. Now the young children are told so much today there is almost no fear in them. This is another thing that makes them think they are fully grown. Some learn sooner than others. Some have to find out the hard way. Things were not told to me about sex or anything about the personal life ahead of me. Now here I was twenty-four, divorced with three children and still a little girl. Oh how I wanted a partner in life. Still at twenty-four I knew so little about life. I married a second time and my new husband helped me grow. Now I was on my way to growing up. Of course then I thought I was already there. I truly was lucky in life. Knowing so little about life, things could have been a lot worse. I still shudder now when I think of how green I was. I can't go back but I can make an effort to help young people realize the consequences of bad choices and that life can be so wonderful if you take care of yourself. It is not easy trying to go the right way when you are so young. Step back, wait. There used to be a saying; stop, look and listen. Trying applying that and it might be beneficial to just see how it turns out for those going the wrong way. Slow down, you have a lifetime to have fun and enjoy life.

I am still enjoying my life. Thank goodness I still am in good health. I still do not smoke or swear, never started it. I do like to have a glass of wine or a nice mixed drink every so often. I just don't over do it.

Here are a few of my observations on teens in love. Oh how their hearts can deceive their minds. The poor little darlings lose all their good sense, if they had any in the first place with that under-developed brain of theirs. When a young person finds their first love they are now in seventh heaven. Oh how grown up they feel. Plus their new love can do no wrong. I truly feel sorry for them. Especially the girls; sorry girls it's true. I had six girls and I know first-hand. Their hormones are racing out of control and their emotions are all over the place. The boys, either with their hormones out of control or unfortunately just wanting to prove they are a man, will tell the girls they love them. The girls, with that inner desire to be loved, plus the hormonal and emotional explosion going on, give in, thinking they will ever meet another that they will love so much. Until the next week when the boy does not call and they see him arm and arm with his new love. Oh I have seen it happen the other way around too; the girls talking the boys into misbehaving. And it is nothing new either. I saw plenty of it happening when I was growing up. Fortunately I was way too green and Grandma made sure I was afraid of doing anything like that. Thanks Grandma. Unfortunately when we let our heart be our guide everyone loses for the most part. The Bible tells us "the heart is treacherous," believe it. Girls get pregnant and the boy says bye-bye. Or maybe they try to do the "right thing" and get married but then you have kids raising kids. I haven't even mentioned all the diseases that you can get. Think before you act, please. Sex is not love people. That goes for young and old. There are so many different kinds of love. Young love, a love between a man and his wife, the love you have for food and for nature, the love you have for your children and grandchildren. All of it is so wonderful and so different. God said love one another.

Do not give up on your kids. Even though you may want to knock the little darling in the head sometimes, your efforts often manifest themselves later. Teach them about God, faith, hope and love. Insist that they use good manners and respect their elders. Stay away from drugs and excessive drinking. Some of my kids had to experiment a little bit after they left home. That is something I simply would not allow. Some escaped with only surface damage. Others suffered effects long after they left that silliness behind. I found plenty of fun things to do without getting into drugs. What a great feeling to wake up with a clear head. They are on their own when they leave so do your best while they are in your control. Our bodies are like automobiles. If we do not maintain them properly they will break down sooner or later. Take care of your beautiful body, keep it clean and shiny inside and out, flush out the dirty gunk regularly and watch out for the potholes. Now is the time to think of your older life. Hopefully you will be in good health.

I simply cannot express this enough about the importance of starting early and teaching your children as they grow. I see so many children headed in the wrong direction and it is very frustrating when all I can do is watch. Some think it is funny and cool to use bad language, and I'm not talking about bad grammar here. If they are taught how the use of bad language makes them sound so immature this would help them in their teens. People that don't use profanity don't really want to be around those that do. Consequently the people you end up having for your friends are the immature potty mouths. Bad language is something I never used and still don't. It is just not necessary. I had my own coin words I used when I was upset like, daggumit, or darn it. A couple phrases I used to express that the kids got a kick out of were, "honest to Pete" and "blame it on to Wilber." One time my youngest son Ted came running in all excited and out of breathe stammering, "LLLLLLorrie said BBBBBBBlame it on to Wilber." Honestly, the kid's never heard me cuss because I didn't. They learned a few words from their dad though. He never mastered the control of his tongue. Nowadays kids think using bad language makes them look grown up. Hey grown-up's, watch your mouth around your kids, and everywhere else for that matter. It's not attractive in the least. It also makes you sound immature and stupid. Is that clear enough? It's very hard for me listening to kids and adults add a bad word in their everyday talk. It changes their looks. I say, "What's the use in using bad words?" You can get your point across without such bad language. There are no bad words in the Bible. Oh, here's a funny story. My Great-Grandson Tommy read the word ass in the Bible so he asked his Grandma if it was okay if he says that, since it was in the Bible and everything. She explained to him if you're talking about the animal then its okay but if you're talking about a person, preferably not. Actually, here's another funny story about using bad language. Well, actually I guess it is more of a confession. One time a cuss word just slipped out of my mouth. I was shocked. Unfortunately for me my Granddaughter Cheri heard me say it. She was shocked too. She said, "Gramma! I never heard you cuss before in my whole life." And then, because one bad thing just happens after another I did the only thing I could do; I lied about it. "No I didn't" just popped out of my mouth. It was too late though, she heard it loud and clear. "Okay, I accidentally said a bad word, big deal, just don't tell anybody," I quickly confessed. Cheri said, "Are you kidding? I am going to tell everybody, they are not going to believe this." Yeah, I'm from the old school. I think a little of the old school would not hurt our young children of today.

I saw something the other day when my son Ed and I were eating at a restaurant. There was this darling little girl, about a year and a half, sitting in a high chair. What a beautiful smile she had. Well evidently she got bored, picked up a butter knife and started to poke her father with it but he just kept dodging her attempts. Oh how I wanted to tell him to tell her to stop. Little children just want to know what they can get away with, just how far they can go. Often they will just keep going until they find the line. Parents please, show your children the line. In short, start young. I can't believe he didn't just take that knife out of her hand and explain to her the inconsiderateness of her actions, let alone the danger. He was probably "giving her some space, letting her express herself as a free-spirit." Man I hate that phrase. I've heard it more than I'll ever want to. He was probably afraid she would throw a fit right there and he didn't want to deal with it. Deal with it parents, right then and there. If they start throwing a fit then you simply just pick them up and take them in the bathroom or out to the car for a little "talk." I'm not trying to sound all great or anything but people actually turned their heads in wonder when Art and I came into a restaurant with eight kids in tow. Boy our kids knew better than to get out of control too. I did my famous squeeze of the leg under the table trick and then they knew they were in trouble. They knew they better not squeal out in pain either, they knew that would only make things worse. This is just what I'm talking about, start young.

Of course teenage time now is so different than in my teenage time or even when my children were teens, from 1925 to 1980. Oh what a rough time for teenagers of today with all the new gadgets for them to play with. It's just one thing after another and a lot of expense for a toy that is upgraded or out of date and ends up being just for a short time of fun. Read a book once in awhile. Go ride your bike. Get off that computer or cel phone or IPOD. Oh if they could only see how small their brains are compared to how big their head is.

Learning takes time. I know I say this plenty of times in this book. I know it sounds like I have been picking on them but I love teenagers. They are very important people in my life. They can be so smart and fun to be around. I have so many. I have actually learned a lot from them. And they have helped me a lot too. Whenever I need help on the computer or my phone or anything like that, bingo, there one is at my door. It's amazing to watch the brain-power at work before my eyes with my kids from about the ages of ten to twenty. After that you are on your way. It's like reading a good book and you want to get to the end fast . . . the raging bull behind the gate at a rodeo, all that energy and knowledge all bottled up inside. Open the gate and watch them fly.

It's so hard to let them go and have most of them turn a deaf ear to your warnings about all the bad things that are out there like don't abuse alcohol, stay away from drugs, eat right, get your sleep, and use your manners. Each little reminder that goes unheeded depletes their bodies of so many things as they age. Once you lose something in your body it's gone. Oh there are replacements for some of the things they need. We are made up of all kinds of different parts but just like a car, when one part goes, everything else starts falling apart. Your bodies need all the help you can give them. Just because we cannot see inside our body does not mean something is not going on in there.

Do not destroy your body while it is still developing. Don't put your life in reverse. I'm not telling you to stop having fun but realize what fun really is. Just be careful and don't go crazy out there. If we let the bad things in life take over our minds and bodies we are in trouble. This is one of the reasons there is so much trouble going on in this old world, troubled minds. Teenagers, listen to me. This is such a wonderful time in your life. You have so much energy to burn and so much excitement to look forward to. Everything is new, it's all up to you, love, laugh, live and grow strong. Here I go again. As I have already said a number of times, learning takes time. I can say that with confidence because I am eighty-five and I am still learning.

There are people in our Government running things, in my opinion mostly the wrong way. They are much more concerned with how things turn out for them than us. They have far too much control over our lives, or so it seems. There are so many people going the wrong way by doing everything for their own gain. Oh I know this book is mostly about young people but young people grow up and become adults. Some grow up faster than their minds develop and then they are immature, underdeveloped adults. Money is the most important thing in their lives. But, that's what people think, in fact, it is a reality. The world revolves around money. Just look at the millionaires in our government, spending their money to get in office, just so they can run your life. There is so much they could do to help; like giving businesses better incentives to stay in this country and not take our jobs overseas. Or, if they take our jobs overseas charge them plenty. They would think twice. Hey, it is their country also, if it goes belly-up where would their millions be? They just don't think it will, but it will and they will be shocked. It would be nice if they would use some of their millions to create work for this country and get us back on track. We need jobs. There are just too many it foolishly and are not held accountable for it and just ask for more. We are not helping them by just handing it out. They actually start thinking so wrong, like we have plenty and we should share it with them. Let them struggle a little. Teach them how to earn it. Unfortunately some parents get the wrong thinking that they want to give their children what they never had. This is good to a certain degree. When the children appreciate and act wisely with what they receive it is good. It is a joy for the parent to help out any way they can, even abundantly if they are in the position to do so. But teach them how to take care of themselves.

There are so many things to do out there today that make us think we are having fun. It is so hard to tell young people there is life after "young life." I have so many grand and great grandchildren where I get a first-hand view of plenty of teenage habits. In addition to the abundance of drugs and alcohol that are available, kids are involved in so many extreme sports and silly stunts that put their lives in so much danger. Sorry to say this but some of the teenagers today are so centered on themselves and think they are invincible. There are many adults out there today suffering from the repercussions of their childish and irresponsible behavior as teens and young adults. Oh how they would like to go back to their younger life and do it over.

One of the main things that troubles young people is finding a new love. Love is so important in their lives. Yes it is important in all our lives but when you are young it seems so urgent to find the right one, right now. Unfortunately if it appears that the one they pick is wrong for them, they go right on to the next person. It takes time to pick the right mate and time to grow together and understand each other. How important love is. I was there. I blinded myself thinking someone was right for me. It took a few years for me to understand the relationship was not right for either of us.

Thank goodness most of my grandchildren are taking care of their lives. This alone gives me so much joy. I have so much love in my life. This is one of the reasons I love writing about young people. They are a great source of joy to me. Because of them I have seen plenty. When I hear older people say "if I could only go back." I say, "No way, are you kidding me, teenage time is too hard, no matter when you were a teenager." In many ways though I still think that today is even harder for young people, there are just too many temptations. I wish more would take the time to wonder what will happen to them if they do not take care of themselves while they are young and developing.

Now there is a pill to help your bones from breaking. But believe me sometimes it's too late. I sure wish there was a pill like that around for my Grandma. Poor thing, she suffered so much. I wonder how long she would have lived with the medications of today. Medications are good if you pay attention and be careful you are actually taking the right thing for you. You are probably best off, if you can, to just eat right, drink plenty of water and exercise. It is healthier on your organs. Exercise and a good attitude go a long way for a healthy brain too. Your brain grows even when you grow old so never quit trying to learn. I am so glad I took on the challenge of learning the computer in my eighties. You kind of have to force yourself sometimes. You will be so glad if you do. There's always something new and exciting to learn if you are not afraid to try. God gave us this beautiful body and free will to develop it. Don't rely on yourself or what other people say too much. He will guide you if you ask. Believe me you cannot go it alone. Sometimes we think we are so in control and away we go abusing what he gave us with bad thoughts and bad habits that deplete our beautiful bodies and minds of vim and vigor. Don't throw away all you have been given just for a short time of crazy fun. Ask anyone who was not given a perfect body what a treasure you have. Do not destroy it for a little hidden fun it will cost you in the long run. There is so much out there to enjoy. Too bad we find out later in life. Some young people, when something does not go their way, grab at straws, anything to have fun, fun, fun. They lose themselves in what makes them happy at the time. They turn into another person. Oh this went on in my day too. But today there are just so many more things to handle. I have seen so much of this. Poor little troubled darlings who got in with the wrong crowd and some made the wrong choices. You have more control than you think for the most part. I'm truly happy I have plenty of grandchildren that are doing great; going about life, working, getting a higher education, loving and caring for themselves and their families. There is only a treasured few that worry me.

Oh they do not realize I can see their bad habits. Someone is always telling me of things the other child is doing wrong. So I just listen. Later on they wonder, "Just how did she know that?" Hey all I have to do is sit back, look and listen. Funny how one child likes to tell me something bad about the other. Hey, look at the scandal sheets, they're always finding bad things about someone; all this does not keep them off the scandal sheet. If only people could see their faults as clear as they see another's. This has been going on since the beginning of time and will go on till the end of time. I constantly have to keep in mind that just because they tell me something bad about another child it does not make it so. Now I watch and learn for myself. I try to think of ways I can help them but it's not very easy for an old lady.

They just think, "You are old, you just don't understand, it's not the same," even if the situation I went through is *exactly* the same. Hey all of you have taught me plenty. I hope you have learned something from me. I have so many children to listen to. Oh what fun I am having watching, learning something new from each one of them. As I said, many things are different than when I was a teenager, I realize that. But some things are just the same.

Kids have so many things handed to them at a very young age. You might be getting tired of hearing this, or think this old lady is just repeating herself over and over like a broken record but it is true, this is one of the reasons our teenagers are having so much trouble; too much too soon. And if you are stuck in the belief that your parents owe you anything beyond teaching you to trust in God, providing you a home, food and clothes you are sadly mistaken. Anything you receive beyond those so-called basics should be considered as a gift. Don't think you are so darn smart because you know a lot more than I did at a young age. We all end up deserving the same thing; love and respect. Now you are in your teens and you want to go out on your own. You think it's time to take care of yourself, good for you. You have a big job ahead of you. It is usually much more than a young person realizes. If you need help from your parents, you are not going it alone. But that's okay, I understand. Asking for a bit of assistance is fine but that is where some humility and respect come in. "Thanks mom, thanks dad, I really appreciate your help and I will repay you slowly but surely." How wonderful it would be to hear that more often. Well parents, teach your children not to just expect a handout. Sometimes parents are in a position that they can help their children more than other parents. If that is the case, please parents, make sure they realize that it isn't something they have coming. Maybe you don't really need for them to pay you back monetarily but if they are offering please find some way for them to repay and learn the value of it. We all need a loan sometimes in our lives. I received a few loans in my time but I always paid them back. Thank goodness I taught my children this. I have been given the greatest gift in life; children that have actually listened and adhered to good advice.

Most of the children of today do not know hard times. Some really don't take the time to stop and think about things reasonably when they have a problem. Hey, stuff happens, everything in life does not always run smooth or go the way we planned. Just deal with it and move on. I didn't expect that the responsibility of taking care of my Grandmother was going to be given to me at thirteen but that's what happened. Not that I would wish that on anyone, let alone a thirteen-year-old but you know, I believe I was actually given a better chance to grow through my Grandma. I had to help her with everything. She taught me plenty. It is kind of sad that I never had a young life or anything fun to do. I sure did like working in my Dad's store though, that was my fun. Oh well, I never had a chance to get into trouble. That was a good thing that came out of all that responsibility. That should teach you parents something. Give your kid a certain amount of responsibility. It will help them grow up and keep them out of trouble. Instill some fear into your kids it's a protection. I was frightened of everything. I agree that my parents and Grandma did go a little overboard but honestly, it helped me more than it hurt me. I love watching all my young people enjoying the fun things they are doing. I'm glad when they choose the right kind of fun because fun is truly what you make it.

I enjoy my old life. My dream was to have a good husband, children, a nice home, oh how I looked forward to this and got it. I did not need someone to help me enjoy my life. Thank goodness for Grandma's help. Learn to love unconditionally, what a different love this is. She taught me how to make myself happy. Happiness is something we have to create for ourselves. Who is going to make you happy when you are alone? Prepare for it and you will be contented. Keep the Lord in your life. What a great helper he is. This way you have someone in your life that will never give you bad advice, never cheat you and always be there to comfort you; with him you are never alone.

What makes one person happy does not make the other person happy. We are all so different from one another no two minds are alike. One of the most gratifying ways to make our own self happy is to make someone else happy. Oh it is so great to make someone happy. Be strong and stick up for the things you know are right. Don't talk that way just because they do. Don't wear those baggy clothes just because they do. Step out of line. Yeah, Grandma is telling you to step out of line. Step out of the assembly line. Don't follow anyone down the stupid road. Hey I know how rough teenage time is, we all need time to enjoy our life. I'm just trying to tell you that you can enjoy life everyday even if it seems there is nothing exciting to do. Make your life special for you. You are the only one that can do that. Your life is up to you. What do you want out of life?

Sit down and make a list. Check that list once in a while and see how you are doing. Don't be surprised when you see how your priorities change.

I am surrounded by teenagers and they keep me alive and happy. I get plenty of fun and laughter just watching them as they grow from adolescent to teen then young adult.

It's like watching a bull enter an arena or a prancing horse in a parade. How they strut and snort and think they have the world by the tail. They don't even realize how much joy they give me, just like I did for my Grandma. I am so happy I was able to bring her joy. I am so happy I have this to remember. We laughed a lot together. I treasure laughing with my children, grandchildren and great-grandchildren. I talk to as many young and older people as I can and have enjoyed relating some of their stories in this book. Knowledge is power they say. Take in as much as you can.

Thinking they are ready for the world the raging bull from within comes out. Watching all these beautiful children grow has taught me plenty. No, we cannot go back but sometimes it feels like I can go back through all my growing children. There is more trouble in the world today. Some of our darling children are confused about what is right for them. More gangs, drugs, alcohol, free sex, cell phones, games to play, everything is so easy to get. Too many older people selling all the things to our young people who want to have a good time. They lose their identity. Look at me, married at twenty and I had three babies by the time I was twenty-four. I truly never had a teenage time. I always thought I was a grown up. Of course I never had all the problems young people have to face today so it was different and it will be different for all their darling children. Things are changing so fast these days. There are so many things to play with. It is so hard to grow up. Oh if they would only listen. They just have so many wants. Watching some of the young people with a cell phone, texting away, not carrying on a conversation with thoughts around them, just like they are in a far away land. I have this with a few of my great grandchildren. So many young people do not know anything about how to work. Yes work

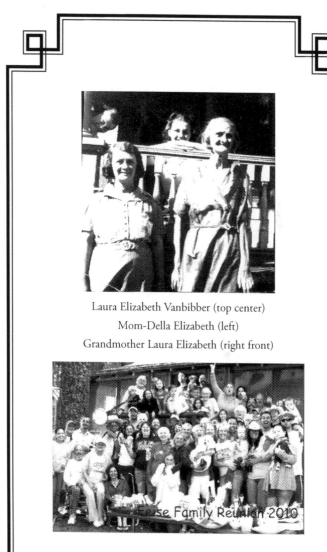

Laura Elizabeth Vanbibber (top center)
Mom-Della Elizabeth (left)
Grandmother Laura Elizabeth (right front)

Feise Family Reunion 2010

HERE ARE A FEW STORIES ABOUT GROWING UP THAT SOME HAVE SHARED WITH ME

MY FIRST YOUNG PERSON RELATES:

"You bet I thought I was ready to go out on my own at fifteen. Let me tell you, my grandma tried to tell me I was not ready. I just thought she was an old lady that did not understand today's world. Well here I am going on forty-eight. Man what I learned in the last thirty-three years. Yes I went to college for a while but I dropped out. I thought I knew enough but oh how little I knew. Now I love to get all the input my Grandma can give me. I did so many things that were not good for my body or my mind. Grandma told me that your mind can get you in plenty of trouble, as mine did. Being the grown-up, as I thought I was, I knew what was good for me. Having fun was so important. Partying was what I wanted to do. It would have been alright if I did not take some of the bad stuff that was not good for me. I really thought I was taking care of myself but Mom and Dad were really taking care of me. 'I'm grown up now,' I thought to myself, 'and it was time to enjoy me own life.' So I took whatever was out there to make me high. After all, I was going to live my own life now and I knew just what was good for me. It got to the point where I never knew what day it was. My good friends and family left me. I lost my beautiful child. I do not even know where she is. She is on my mind all the time. Oh how I wanted to quit this awful stuff. I cried so much when I was alone. Good thing I had God in my life. I finely turned back to him. Now I do not have the need for that bad stuff. Believe me it took its toll on me. I try now to help young people to understand that if you start with all the terrible stuff that is out there, there's no turning back. But you can start over as I did. What a wonderful life I have now. Like Grandma said, 'Jesus told us in the Bible that all we have to do is listen.' Now I'm back on a straight way of life. So many years I spent in needless suffering. Yes I know where I went wrong. Plus I thought I knew what was good for this smart kid. Listen to someone older, it can help you later. I am now enjoying my life with a new wife and children. Thank goodness God gave me another chance. He gave me plenty of chances; I just did not recognize them at such a young age. I'm just hoping my lost daughter can forgive me. I know I have to forgive myself. Being young is a hard time in your life because we think we know what is good for us and it is so important for us to go wild and have a good time as we see it. I am so happy I woke up. Yes it's like I was sleepwalking as I look back. I know there is so much more I will learn. There is happiness after young time. I am much more in tune with myself. The best part is now I can go and make someone else happy besides myself."

ANOTHER STORY:

"It was hard for me to grow up. I was taken care of all my life. When the time came for me to go out on my own it was not easy. At nineteen I was going to college and thought, "Now I am grown up,' or so I thought. I truly did not know which way to go. 'You bet,' I thought, 'I can take care of this smart kid.' I had a few different jobs and hated them all. I was more interested in having fun. I never paid any attention to what was going on around me. Now at my older age boy how different life is for me. The little college education I had did not help much. I am now taking care of myself and starting a new family. Mom and Dad always told me to listen to what Jesus told us in the Bible but this was for someone else, not me. He said listen to what I tell you. Now I hear him. My teenage years were supposed to be full of fun as I saw it. No one else mattered as long as I was enjoying my life. I lost a beautiful love because of my bad habits. Thank God I grew up and turned back to God's guidance. I found a new love, which I thank God for. No way would I want to go back to my teenage life. You are right Grandma. I am so happy I have you in my life. You are my hindsight."

HERE ARE A FEW THOUGHTS AS I REMEMBER MY LITTLE BROTHER BOBBY

On November 27, 1935 my Dad called my brothers Warren, Charlie and me into the living room. He brought out a basket and said he wanted to show us something. I looked in and said, "A baby?" Everyone laughed. Here I was ten years old and not even knowing that we were going to have a new baby in our home. Yes, I still thought they came in with the doctor's black bag! Little Bobby was a treasure to all of us. He used to come in my Dad's furniture store and visit me when I was working. I left home when he was ten so he never really got to know me. I took him to his first day of school; the roads were covered with snow. I was fifteen. I kept up on his life through our mother. She filled me in on what he was doing. Bobby was a mild-natured young man. He always listened to Mom and Dad.

HERE IS WHAT BOB RELATES ABOUT HIS LIFE:

"I had a very good young life. I was the youngest of nine. By the time I was a teenager all my siblings left home, it was as if I was an only child. We never had much but I always thought we had plenty. I truly never got into trouble thank goodness. One of the things I remember was talking to Dad about moving to California where my sisters Lela and Laura, nicknamed Lolly, lived. I had dreams of picking an orange off a tree, seeing the ocean and so many new fruits and vegetables. I never even heard of an avocado before. I saw my first live lobster at Fisherman's Wharf when I went fishing with Laura and her husband Art. Laura caught a stingray in the San Francisco bay. What fun I had that day. On our way out to California we had several mishaps. One was in Vendover, Utah. A bearing went out in our truck and it set us back two days. After that, away we went. Then at one point I was riding in the back of the truck on a very rough road. Dad hit a rough spot and I flipped out of the truck. I was not hurt but I had to whistle loud enough for Dad to hear me. We didn't stay in California long before we moved back to Omaha. I love reminiscing. Young people of today have a very hard time adjusting to life. There are too many things they can get without earning a thing. I am so happy my parents made me work because it helped me in my older life. I'm just getting to know my sister Laura, Lolly. Here I am seventy-five years old."

ANOTHER STORY:

"Being a teenager was the most wonderful time for me. My parents bought me a car when I was in high school but I had to work and pay for it. I worked at small jobs. All I paid for was my car and insurance. They took care of everything else. I had plenty of money; some of it I saved, most of it I spent. Working and homework kept me out of trouble. I had plenty of fun with my friends. We all worked and never hung around with kids that took drugs. We liked a few beers once in a while and just knew where we could get it. Mom and Dad never knew until we were older and I told them. Now I look back and laugh at the funny things we thought we were getting away with. I did a few wrong things, running through red lights, speeding, talking loud, telling foul stories and using bad words. I never would say them in front of my parents though. I did like running around with girls that liked to have a good time. I wanted to belong so I went along. This is the trouble with all teenagers; they want to belong. So now I tell them to watch who you hang around with because if you hang with the kids that take the bad stuff and do crazy things just to belong you will suffer for it. Believe me, so will you. It is much easier to be older. Now I have a family to take care of. Having teenagers makes me look back on myself. I understand how they feel. There are so many things out there now, that is the trouble being a teenager of today. Back then we had only just begun to learn what life is all about. My wife and I are doing everything in our power to guide our children in the right direction. Believe me this is not an easy thing for a parent because teenagers think they know all there is to know about life. Now I know how my parents felt. I'm sure happy I had to go to church. I believed in God but I still went a little off course. That is the way it is when you are young; you think you can do no wrong. Thank the Lord I did not step in too many potholes. Like Grandma always said, 'Watch where you step, there may be something you sure wished you did not step into.' Now Grandma and I have a good laugh when one of the teenagers tells us they are not doing anything wrong and we know different. I try to guide them in the right direction. Some listen, some just go their own way. It's just as hard to be a grown-up and watch your children go out on their own. Remember what the Lord told us in the Bible. The Lord has told us how to treat others. The Lord's Prayer tells it all. I read the Bible to my children every day. I'm hoping some of it sinks in. You want them to enjoy their young life. Nothing in life is easy for young or old. All we can do is listen to what Jesus told us in the Bible. I tell them to take care of what God gave you. Do not destroy what God gave you just for a little crazy fun. Funny, after reading what I wrote, I realize I sound just like Grandma. I guess this means I have grown up.

THIS STORY IS FROM A MAN OF SEVENTY-TWO YEARS OLD

"My young years were a terror to my parents. No one could tell me I was doing anything wrong. You better believe I knew it all at a very young age, as I thought. I have two children running around that do not know me because I walked away from their mothers many years ago. You can believe I thought I was having fun. Of course I was. I loved bullying all the other kids around because this made me feel important and bigger than they were. Now I have so many regrets that I cannot do anything about. I married in my wild days. That never worked out. I became a big businessman and made plenty of money. I had everything a person could want. But even my business partners didn't want to have anything to do with me because everything had to go my way. No matter what, I was always right. Now I'm alone with no children to visit or anyone for that matter. Tell me I was having fun growing up. As I see it now, what I lost was more than I gained. The money I have is nothing compared to my losses. I am a very lonely old man and yes it has been my own fault. So you young people out there had better listen up because what you do now will come back to haunt you in your later life. I am haunted, but fortunately for me though, I have found a wonderful person to talk to now and this helps me to endure my old age. We all need someone to talk and laugh with. This is something no one can do alone. Think before you do while you are young."

My neighbor Dorothy Mac Rea is ninety years old. She was born in 1920. I wrote her story in my last book. Well, I misspelled her name along with a few other incorrect details. I rushed that book. I had a tumor removed from my brain and things were not right for me for a year and

41

a half. I needed help with everything. I lost everything I wrote in my computer. I thought I would be able to rewrite what I lost. So I rewrote it. There were so many mistakes. I truly was not ready for anything like that but now I guess my saying applies to me; too much, too soon. So I am going to take another shot at it.

HERE IS DOROTHY'S STORY:

"My young life was entirely different than today's young people. So many new things the young people have to deal with. Young people are in trouble today. They need so much excitement, so many drugs that are easy to get. Once they start taking these bad things they need more. Some get hooked right away. One thing I remember about children in my day is we never talked back, even if we wanted to. Our parents were in control, thank goodness. They taught us to think of others besides ourselves. This is the number one thing young people need today. Some young people of today think they should have everything going their way. Oh some young people in my day went the wrong way. I guess that's the way life is. Everything does not run smooth. Truly I am happy I'm not a teenager today. Now in my older life as I am trying to get up out of my chair I sound like Lawrence Welk with the 'one and a two and a three.' In my first career I went to the Stanton School of Beauty. Then I went on to be a secretary. I married Ray Witherill. Ray worked with Western Machinery in Palo Alto. We moved around quire a bit. I met so many wonderful people in our travels. At one point we transferred to Aurora, Illinois. In 1969 Ray passed away with cancer. I thought my life was over but I had to go on. Years later I married Boyton Mac Rae. I was really blessed to have had two wonderful men in my life. Mac's children are my children. We retired in Florida. Mac passed away with a massive heart attack. It's hard to watch someone die and there is nothing you can do to help them. I drove all the way to Redding, CA from Florida alone. Now I live alone doing my own house and yard work, but lately though I have been giving up some of that work to someone younger. I still get my hair and nails done once a week just for me. I no longer drive as my eyesight will not allow it. Fortunately for me there is a bus available for seniors at a reasonable cost. I lost my sister Ruby Lee a few years back. It's hard to go on when so many loved ones are gone. Thank goodness I have my sister Ruby Lee's daughter Mary to help me with my errands. So many different things you have to endure as you get older. I am enjoying my older life even though I cannot do much. I am still enjoying the time I have."

ANOTHER STORY:

"My young life was great. I enjoyed so much fun. My parents took me everywhere they went. We traveled a lot. I have been all over Europe. I have learned so much from all the different ways and religions I was exposed to. This made me think I was grown up. My Dad was in the Army and we traveled with him. I truly grew up fast. You can bet I was ready to go out on my own as a teenager. Now what a hard time I had on my own. Thank goodness for my parents help after I was on my own. I married a great man, I thought. When our baby entered my life well, this darling man I love so much left me. No baby for him and away he went. To tell you the truth I did not want my baby either but my Mother said I had to keep this child because it was her grandchild. Thank goodness for my mother's help. I am now a Grandma myself. Oh what I would have missed in life. When I went out on my own I wasn't as smart as I thought I was. I did get the change to do so many things other people did not get a chance to do. But like my mother said, 'there is so much we have to learn as we grow.' Now I think differently, what a wonderful life I have now, enjoying my grandchild; lucky me."

ANOTHER STORY:

"I was adopted. My father died young so I never knew him. I was lucky to have my mother as we were very close. I never felt like I was adopted. In my teenage time well, I went out on my own or I should say I moved in with my boyfriend at the time. Now I know how bad that was. He was a lot older than me. I thought I knew just how good this was for me. Everything had to go his way. Boy did I learn how much I needed to take care of me. This was a hard relationship to get out of. I was lost. I took all kinds of bad drugs to forget my problems. Wow, now I was in trouble. My problems were still there. The drugs did not help and only made the problems larger. What a loss for me. Now how was I going to help myself? Thank goodness my mother stood by me. Lucky me, someone in my life loved me. I was helped to get my life back together. God entered into my life again. Oh I knew about God's love before but never thought I needed him. Believe me you need God in your life every day. So he is here to stay in my life. I am too old to have children now. Thank God I have somebody to give me love. Think before you do anything so you do not have to suffer in your older life. I beg God to help me to endure the things that trouble me about my younger life. Thank goodness for my mother's love and forgiveness. Oh how she tried to help me but I knew what was best for me. I am getting closer each day with God's help."

ANOTHER STORY:

"I lived a strange life. My parents never knew I was Gay. Let me tell you how hard this was for me. A few of my friends knew I was Gay. I really kept it to myself. My mother kept bugging me to have a girlfriend, her not knowing I was Gay. When I was thirty years old one of my female friends pretended to be my girl friend and this satisfied my mother. I had to move out of our home to live the life I needed. I still kept this a secret. It was very hard to live this way. It was hard for me to have fun with anyone. I knew I needed to get this out in the open. I never got into trouble as a teenager because I never went anywhere. Now I am in my sixties. My mother is gone. Actually I am enjoying my older life. I live alone. Teenage time was too hard for me. I didn't have anyone to tell my troubles to. Thank goodness I have this wonderful female friend to talk to. We go places together so there's plenty of laughter in my old life. Another good friend, thank you for keeping my secret, is a good friend of my mother's and mine. He helped me to talk to God. I wish I knew him in my teens. Teenagers out there had better listen. Oh how he helped me. When you are troubled give it to him. Now I realize I am loved. Everyone needs love in their life. Thanks for the love of God; he loves us all the same."

These people telling their stories of their young life are trying to help young people to understand that you can enjoy your young life, all you have to do is listen to someone who has been there and done that. This is just what Jesus told us in the Bible, all you have to do is listen. I know how hard this is for young people. They are just beginning to have fun as they see it. Here I go again with all these grandchildren, nieces and nephews that are doing great. I love watching them grow. Here are a couple of stories from my young ones.

A STORY FROM ONE OF MY LITTLE GREAT GRANDDAUGHTERS, ELIZABETH JAYDE SCORDEL, NICKNMAMED LOVEY, AGE SIX:

"I like to come to Grandma GG's because it is fun painting rocks with her. I get to play with her toys. She has all kinds of toys for us to play with. I like her doll that she let me name. I named her Ramona. Grandma GG gave me some jewelry that I could play with and she pierced Ramona's ears so I could put earrings in them. She let me name her other dolls too. Sometimes we bake. I like to dust too. There is always something fun for us to do. Tonight I am spending the night. We are going to make dinner together and then I get to paint a butterfly on the rock I picked out. I don't know what I want to be when I grow up. Sometimes I think I would like to be a teacher. I do very well in school. I have a brother Tommy. Sometimes he gets to come over to Grandma GG's with me. My brother Tommy and I like to go over to our Grandma and Grandpa's house (my daughter Arlene and her husband Mel}. We take turns every other weekend and we sure look forward to it. I told some of my friends at school about our visits and they told me how lucky I am to have so many Grandmas and Grandpas. I love visiting with my other Grandma Suzanne and Grandpa Lloyd. They are my Dad's parents."

THIS IS A STORY FROM MY GREAT GRANDDAUGHTER ALLY CRAIN AGE TEN:

"I used to be around Grandma GG a lot until we moved to Klamath Falls, Oregon. Now we visit her when we come down. My Grandma Lorrie and GG came up for a visit. My mother took pictures of our fifth generation. My sister Kaylea's baby is the fifth one. I am an Aunt to my sisters baby Blakeleigh. I was there the day she was born. I was also with my Mom when my little sister Brooklyn was born. GG said that things were so different when she was my age. I do get a kick out of what she told me about when she was my age and she thought babies came in a little black bag. I did not tell her I thought she was dumb. She sure learned plenty after she grew up. This shows me what I will learn as I grow. I love coming down visiting my family. We always have so much fun having parties. I love my family. They are so much fun. I just love visiting my family. I would love to move back to California and be with my family again. GG said she would like it if I stayed a child but I want to grow up."

Sometimes when I start writing I rattle on and on too much because I have plenty to tell. Oh how much love I have with my darling children, my gift from God. This is not a perfect world. We all make mistakes we would like to correct. We just have to take the bitter with the sweet. There will always be good and bad on this earth for now. It is up to all of us to make the good win. I love it when I see young people having fun, laughing and enjoying their friends. There is nothing better for me. I only had a couple of friends in school. I was an average to above average student and reading was my passion. I was very shy which made me feel so different from all the kids and I often felt alone. I never had friends after school either, that was work time. Consequently my brothers Warren and Charley were pretty much my only friends and we worked together after school until I was thirteen. I just never had all that junk or peer pressure to deal with. I stepped in a few potholes when I thought I was grown up. This I call learning along the way. I was too busy working as a young child to get in any trouble. I'm glad I did. What a love of life I have now. We all have different minds one from another. No two minds are alike. Things are going on the same as in my day, way back when.

ANOTHER STORY:

"I hated my young life. My Mom and Dad divorced when I was in my teens. That was a very hard life for me. I was very close to my Dad but I never got to see him much after the divorce. My mother tried to help me but no way, I was unhappy. So away I went. I left school and went to work at a little job thinking I was taking care of little ole' me. I smoked, drank and swore and took everything I could get my hands on. My problems got bigger and bigger. Somebody had to stop me. I was headed for disaster. Thank goodness I was sent to a group home for about a year. I learned about God and now he is in my life. I wish he was there for me when I was young. Young people of today think life is different from yesterday. The only difference is the ways, saying and new things to play with. Really, I went through too much too soon. Now I am enjoying my life so much. No matter what you are you are only as big as your mind is. Believe me its not very big. When you are a teenager it has to grow to be any good. Now I am in my seventies and my mind is still growing."

I need to express my feelings about Bullies. I heard on TV the other day that a man got on a school bus to confront a bully that was tormenting his daughter. Oh how I knew how he felt. When my brother Warren, who was eight, Charley was seven and I was nine, a bully tormented us everyday on our way to school. Our mother talked to his parents to no avail. One day I came home with my face all scratched and blood all over. That bully hit my brother Warren because he would not do what he wanted. So I hit him. He in turn scratched my face. My mother took care of me while I fainted. Boy was she upset. She took the razor strap to Warren and told him he had to fight the bully.

We were always told never to fight. He never bothered us again. What a hard thing to see my brother fighting with someone. There will always be bullies in life that will try to push you around or say bad thing about you. This young bully was always in trouble with his parents. On Saturdays we could see him running down the street, his dad running after him, and he would be laughing saying, 'catch me if you can Dad.' As I see it today it was his dad's fault for letting him get away with his actions. Young children know what they can get away with at a very young age. It is no different today, talk is cheap. Some people like pointing their finger at someone else to cover up their mistakes. You have to go on and try and ignore their bad habits, which is something hard to do. Bullying should never be tolerated. Bullies should be punished right away. Home, school and on the bus, yes the bus driver can see what is going on. I said this in my other book about a sweet little friend we had. He was always dirty, never had enough clothes to look good and all the other kids laughed and tormented him. Warren, Charley and I protected him. He died of a rat bite in his own home. He finally had some nice clothes to wear. Unfortunately he was in his coffin. There have been bullies since the beginning of time. Remember the story of David and Goliath? Remember what happened to him? I love writing about life. So much is still the same as time goes on, just different sayings, actions and ways. Do not let a bully take over your life. There are good ways to stop them. Hey one older man wrote in this book about his bullying days and how sorry he was. See, they know what they are doing. He would have been happy today if someone would have tried to stop him then.

One of the most difficult things to deal with is sex. This is permitted and parents give their children birth control so as to avoid early or unwanted pregnancies. We never even used the word pregnant. When I was young you were, in the family way.

Sex was an unfamiliar word to me. Some unfortunately feel it is okay to give the child up to be adopted, after all, they reason, there are plenty of people who would love to have a baby and can't. Sadly some feel it is okay to have an abortion. They are so confused. What happened to teaching them to be married first? Sex is not love.

Men and women think differently. I have a bird's eye view of the men and women growing up around me. God made each one so different. I am so happy we are not the same. I get a lot of enjoyment by just watching and listening and yes knowing the answer to plenty of their problems. Oh I try to help some. I sneak a few words in without them realizing I'm trying to help. Nothing in this life is easy. Everything takes work on both sides. No one should be as important as your partner. If each gave to the other what a pleasant relationship they would have. Marriage is a two-way street and there are plenty of stop signs. Just be aware of what you say because your words can come back to haunt you. A phrase I hear that is such a cop out is "just kidding." So that makes it all right to say anything you want? How about, "you never help out." Come on now, never? Try to rephrase that. Recognize what your partner does do whether they work in the home or outside the home. If a woman stays home and takes care of the home she has a big job. It's not a regular nine to five. When five o'clock rolls around that is usually her cue to start dinner, feed the family, help the kids with their homework, bath the kids and put them to bed. If the husband works outside the home, his day is usually finished when he gets home. Or maybe it's not. Maybe he has to do some yard work or chop some wood or work on the car. They both may just have a little time to spend together alone before it's time to go to bed and try to get some sleep before the next day starts all over. All I'm saying is it takes work on both sides. Help each other you guys. Recognize the things your partner does do instead of criticizing them for what they don't do. Try to understand what they are talking about. I see so many times each one wants to be the controller. Remember, a car only has one steering wheel. Somebody has to drive. Each need to find what they are good at being in charge of and share the load.

One of the reasons I married so many times is I have always wanted a partner, someone to laugh with. Sometimes being alone is so hard to handle. When my first husband came into my life I thought he was the most fantastic man, so mature, so worldly, after all he was twenty. As it turns out though he was the same as me, not grown up. Oh I thought he was, all grown up so I leaned on him too much. He said he would help me understand all I needed to know about life. We married and rented a one-bedroom house. We were both working so we had plenty of money. Our first year was great. Then I go pregnant, or "in the family way" as Grandma would have said. Our trouble was just beginning. Now things changed very quickly. We went from a two-income household to one income. Then that didn't last long either. He started drinking pretty heavy. I blinded myself to all the problems that were happening because it was too hard for me to face. I was all ready to be a wife and a mother but that is not what he wanted. Besides, divorce was just not something that was done in my family. I received no help from my family or his. My family told me that I made my own bed and now I needed to sleep in it. His family refused to see reality and thought the problem the time. That is what marriage is supposed to be all about; giving to each other. Marriage is a give and take situation. It seems like sometimes you give more than you get back. The person you choose to marry thinks they know just what kind of person you are, and you are convinced you know this person to the core, but it isn't until after you are together for a while that each of you starts to see just what kind of person they married. Our hidden thoughts, our selfishness, loving deeds, the way we care about others; these thing are all revealed sooner or later. Everyone can see our funny ways better than we can. Because we cannot see our own faults our partner lets us know the things we cannot see. Hopefully this is done in a kind and respectful way. We do well to take constructive criticism with a grain of salt and use it to our advantage. Marriage makes you look at yourself. It opens your mind to yourself. If you are not so set in your ways or think you are perfect, you and you marriage will prosper. Hopefully if you do have something of a negative nature to say to your partner you will talk to them about it in private. I have watched some young couples saying bad things about the other. They hurt their partner by airing their funny ways instead of praising them for something they did well. There are so many good things we can say about our partner. This keeps love alive. So many times we sabotage a very good relationship. Men and women are as different as night and day. God made us to be together. We need each other. This makes the world go round and round. It is the same in every generation, just different ways and sayings. New things are added to make the next generation think they are smarter. Sorry honey, we all come into this world knowing nothing. We learn along the way. Sometimes for some unknown reason, one person is unhappy with the other. Maybe they said something the wrong way or in a certain tone of voice that sets us off. Maybe they didn't even realize how it sounded. It's all about our mind. How you react could make all the difference. This is what I'm talking about. This will go on until the end of time. Our thoughts are all so different. No two minds are alike. When you feel unhappy with the relationship, first and foremost, stop and talk to your partner. You wanted them at one time in your life. You thought you learned so much about them. Now you think differently? Sometimes this is the time you are just starting to know them. Give things a chance. You both need time to adjust to each other. This is what is called learning along the way. We each have a different thing we want in life. Didn't you want this person in your life? Well my dear the person you wanted is now in your life. Some are unhappy with their new partner and want out. Sometimes it's too late. Oh how sad for not taking the time to talk. Men or women, it does not make any difference. No one on this earth is perfect. You will never find a perfect person. It's all in your mind. What do you want in a person, someone who will act and think the same as you? Sorry honey, there is no such person. So take the time to understand the person you chose to share your life with. Give them time to develop into the person you want to spend the rest of your life with. As I said, it is up to each one. We all need someone to love and care about us. This is life. Think before looking for that perfect person. When we marry we feel we found that person. Then, sometimes, we feel we made a mistake, that person we chose is not the person we want to spend the rest of our life with. Come on wake up. Think. Give the one you love a chance. Show them love. This is all they want.

Oh how much of this I have seen. Believe me, if you would only listen. Just like Jesus said in the Bible. Oh I know some people do not believe but thank goodness I believe. Oh how this has helped me through so many things I could not do anything about. I had someone to give my troubles to. Hey, we cannot go it alone. There's help if we ask for it. We all need spiritual guidance. This is the reason we need Jesus. I am so thankful my Grandma helped me to understand how much Jesus would help me, if I just let him. He will help you with all your troubles but you have to work with him. This has helped me get through so many rough spots. I paid attention to Grandma and I grew. I talk to Jesus every day. Keep him at your side. He is your personal savior. He has a source of power that is unmatched. Use it. We are all important and loved by God and his son Jesus. Enjoy what he gave you. Living to eighty-six and having this abundance of family, it really gave me chance to understand what Jesus is trying to tell us in the Bible. You can't go wrong learning what is in the Bible and listening to his advice. You were given a body, a mind and free will. Use it wisely. Follow his advice.

I always wanted a partner in life. I did not like living alone. So, I chose to have a partner to be with. I gave with my whole heart. I had to remember they had to give also. It's important to know when to stick up for yourself too. This is what marriage is all about; give and take. We are not always right. I always gave more than I received. So try to listen to the one you chose for your life partner. Just think you might be the problem. It is so great to have someone to talk to. It is very hard to laugh alone. So don't make life hard for yourself. Think of someone other than yourself. Try very hard to think of what the other person would like once in a while. It's all about blending your lives together. Make it right for both of you. Do not let anyone mistreat you. Just because you are not happy in a relationship it doesn't mean you should just pick up and go. Think before you do anything. This is what marriage is all about. Sometimes giving up some of your freedom or having to do things a bit different than you are used to is worth it. Now you have what you have been looking for, someone to share your life with. Make it fun and exciting; take care of what you have. Don't look for someone better. It takes time to see through the one you love. We are blind when we love someone. We cannot see their faults plus we all change as we grow. We all change differently. This is where the trouble begins. Sometimes these changes hurt a marriage. Give your love to your partner. This is one of the greatest gifts in a relationship. Love is not just sex. Love is listening, doing things for each other, caring, growing together, talking, laughing, crying, holding hands, cuddling, telling each other something personal. Keep your relationship alive. Take care of this important love. Greet each other with a hug and a kiss when you have been away for a while. We all change as we grow so grow together. This is what makes love grow. Most of the time it does not make any difference who is right or wrong. You can't be right all the time. So get to work now. Tomorrow may be too late. It's a wonderful world. It's all in how you choose to live in it.

Does anyone remember this saying, "The grass is always greener?" It is so sad when one of the marriage partners is unhappy with their relationship and they step out of line. Too bad, now they are going into the same situation of starting a new relationship and not knowing what the other person is really like. Sometimes you wonder "what have I done?" But sometimes it is good to leave a disturbed, abusive, lazy, drug or alcohol induced person. Now you have to start a new life. Believe me it can be done. Sometimes someone else enters their life that brings back that first love so you step out of line. Love is so strong it can take over your thoughts or good senses. So now take time to think of what you are doing. A new relationship, oh how you might enjoy this new love for a while. Then, your mind wakes up a little into this new situation. Now what do you do? Sometimes it's hard to go back, even if you or your partner and you want to reconcile. All I'm trying to tell each and everyone is to think before you decide to leave. Use that beautiful brain you were given. There are so many reasons to leave this I realize. But now, do not make your life miserable with thoughts of something better. Put your efforts of a good life to work for yourself and your partner. Believe me; now that I am older I can see how trouble starts. Some married people forget to say I love you. They take their loved one for granted, never seeing anything they do for the good. Take care of that special person you chose, there is nothing better out there. It will not matter to anyone in this world but you. We all have our own thoughts. Be honest and open, talk to each other, and communicate. What a wonderful relationship you can have if you open your life to your loved one. Everyone's thoughts are so different from one another; this is the reason we need to talk to each other to find out what they are thinking. Take the time to find out the things they like or different things they like to do. Listen to each other. Life is different than when I was young. Now there are too many things to entertain us with. We lose sight of that person we chose. So let someone that has seen so much and continues to see what is happening out there give you a little advice. It just might help. What a treasure to find someone we can spend our life with. This is one of the things most of us look forward to, finding a partner and a home of our own.

Love people, not money. Too many love money and forget the one they love. Being content is very important. If you are not content this brings trouble. Resist the urge to compare yourself with others because you are special. Maintain an appreciate attitude. Sometimes we forget to appreciate our partner. It is very important to choose your friends wisely because you will do what they do, good or bad. Take good care of your spiritual life, you are the only one that can do that. We all need spiritual guidance. This is the reason we need Jesus.

If we applied these things with our partners we would find love. Yes, I will say this a number of times but I am just trying to get my point across how important we all are to each other. We could save ourselves plenty of heartache. I want to help people to understand what is going on in their life. Life is so complicated. So many things we have to learn along the way. This is the hard part, learning.

When you are a teenager you think you know it all and are ready to go out on your own just because you are as big as your parent. Sorry honey. You are just beginning to learn how life is going to treat you. Oh how hard this is for a young person, marriage. It is hard to understand another person when you are just beginning to understand yourself. Now it is up to you to listen to someone who has been there and done that and found out the mistakes they made. Believe me; you will go in a much better direction. I know, I know, this is hard for anyone to hear. It's all up to each of us.

Losing loved ones is probably the hardest thing anyone will go through. I lost three husbands to cancer. I never thought I would marry so many times. My Grandmother, Mother, Father, four sisters; Lela, Mary, Betty and Teddy, my brothers Al and Charley, have all gone. My little three year old Great-Grandson drowning was a horrible tragedy. It is very hard to lose someone you love, especially if it is your child. I had to watch helplessly as my sweet daughter June died of a Parkinson's related disease at the young age of 54. My son-in-law died of a heart attack at the age of forty-five. We all live a short time on this earth that God gave us to enjoy. One day will come when there will be no more death for any of us. Someday we will all meet again. Now I live alone. So much you have to cope with as you get older and are still around. It is sometimes very hard for the living.

Sometimes it is not easy to get old when you don't hear from your loved ones. You can get so lonely when you live alone. Life takes on different meaning. Now this is the time you really should be thinking of yourself. I am so happy I found things to keep me contented. Writing is one of the things that keep me going. Oh yes, I paint rocks for little children. My home looks like a child lives here with all the toys, books and games all over. I just feel good with these things around. So many older people do not have a family around so they just live day to day. I heard so many older ones say they do not want to live to be one hundred, what for? Frankly neither would I, even though I have so many things in my favor. One of the main things an older person needs to realize is you cannot do the things you used to. You can hurt yourself for one. Then you would be in a lot worse shape. Another is you can get so down about things. Sometimes we feel so useless, especially if you were an active young person. Believe me this is not a good feeling. But I do know how lucky I am and I try to keep myself contented. I know it is only up to me. Truly I live a fantasy life. I do not act like I'm old. You are as young as you feel. Just remember all you young people life is what you make it, young or old.

I make my life full of excitement. I love making someone else happy, this keeps me happy. I feel I was given so much. I'm thankful for what I received.

First and foremost my teenage life is way behind me. Now life is so much different. Of course I know more about what to do and how to take care of myself but now that I have the time and can do anything I want to I simply do not have the energy. I can't stand very long. Some mornings I am full of ambition and energy but it runs out so quick. Life is so different for me now. I love reminiscing. Now I could care less how long it takes to do anything. Now I have to sit down sooner. I enjoy reading the Bible over a second cup of coffee. Thank God I have some energy left. Of course I never knew what it would be like when I got old. Life can actually be rough at anytime in your life but it is always up to you to find something you can enjoy that is safe and legal. Old or young each have their own set of problems. So please listen up. Give yourself a chance to grow, to understand that you really do not know much about life because it takes a lifetime to learn. Listen to someone who knows what they are talking about; a voice of experience. Now I enjoy my life through my children and grandchildren and great grandchildren. I even have great great grandchildren. Their fun and laughter gives me fun and laughter. The young people don't realize how hard it is not to be able to do the things you used to. I know this is hard for them to understand. I have been through plenty of the same things they are going through today. The clown in me comes out every once in a while. I know they look at me sometimes and wonder if I am every going to grow up. Sorry darlings, no I won't. Hey, I became a clown for children's parties when I was sixty-two. Many of my grandchildren joined me on this adventure. We all dressed up like clowns and were in several parades. We won a few ribbons and trophies. What fun I had. How wonderful to be young and have so much energy and ambition. Raising a family takes so much out of you. I still get knots in my stomach when any of my children or their children does something that is not good for them. That's a lot of knots. You need to have a good job to provide a good home and take the children all the places they need to go. You have to have a lot of energy and patience to teach them all they need to know and all they need to be aware of. Hopefully you have a little energy left to enjoy yourself. Yes, I was there. Oh how busy I was and my family always came first, even if they didn't realize it. Truth be known they never gave me much trouble. Everyone will get old someday, that is, if you live long enough. I always took care of everything I needed to do and now I have to ask for help and that is hard for me to do. I know what it is, pride. Oh how that stupid pride gets in the way. But I can't shake it. I am so happy I can do something that keeps me happy. Oh how different it is now. I am happy just to wake up and do what I can. I am very thankful that my children call and stop by. My life moved so fast without me even realizing it. My trouble is now I can't do half the things I used to when I was young. I still want to work. There are so many things you cannot do even though you still want to do everything for yourself. Oh, I haven't given up just yet but I am beginning to know just what I can and can't do. Fun and laughter isn't really something you can do alone but when I am alone I like to keep all the young children's faces and sayings in my mind. It makes me laugh to myself and it keeps me young at heart and in my mind. There are all kinds of happiness. The fun I have in my later life now is due to my family and friends. Oh what fun I have been having watching them grow.

I have learned so much from my beautiful family. Each one taught me something different. Life takes on a different meaning as you get older. You need so many different things to enjoy. My darling son Ed comes to lunch every Wednesday and he takes me to church on most Sundays. He also brings me flowers every so often. Arlene, Tree, that's Elaine, and her husband Steven, Lorrie and Mike are always here. I see Shirley and Diana a little less often but they don't live close by. They call me and we have some nice conversations. I see Don several times a week and enjoy our visits. Ted and Gene live in Oregon so I don't get to see them as often as I would like. Everyone is always there whenever I need them. You can bet I need them plenty too. Someone is always dropping by. Nora and Glenda call and check on me on a regular basis. I have truly been blessed as life goes on for me with all my darling children, grandchildren, great grandchildren, great-great grandchildren, nieces, nephews and friends. I just turned 86 in March and I am still the baby in my group of friends. Some things just never change. My good friend Virginia McComb just passed away, she was ninety. My neighbor Dorothy Mac Rea is ninety, Erv Kolbe is ninety-seven and his wife Noreen is eighty-eight. Virginia Meadow is eighty-seven and Ruth C is ninety-three. All these people had a great young life and are now enjoying their older life.

This family was one of my fondest dreams and God gave me what I asked for. My family tree is like a mighty oak with so many branches, all going in different directions. What a magnificent group of people I have in my life, such diversity. I have just about every nationality and religion and that makes for some interesting conversations sometimes. What fun it is for me listening to everyone, each with their own thoughts and ways. I try to listen to all of them patiently. We all dance to a different drummer. This was God's intent when he gave us free will. Unfortunately some see this as having the liberty to go our own way and make up our own mind as to what is right and what is wrong and go about as they see fit. That's not the way it is. Some like to say bad things about one another. Too bad they can't see themselves. Now that I'm older I notice how many see the bad things more than the good. They just make themselves look bad in my eyes. It's too bad they choose the bad things because no one is perfect. Having so many children to take care of, trying to teach them to love, live right, and take care of themselves was quite a job, especially for a shy person such as me. I definitely lost my shyness as I grew. One of my favorite things I enjoyed doing for my children was cooking. Dinner was my favorite meal because that was the one time we were all at the same place at the same time. I got particular enjoyment out of this because for the most part they liked everything I prepared. What fun I had watching their smiling faces as they ate. I never had much to give them but they never went hungry and it was very rewarding to see them clean their plates. I generally tried to prepare some sort of dessert for them as well. I couldn't give them a lot of toys but I could certainly keep them well fed. I guess that was of high importance to me because my parents struggled to keep all of us just fed. I still love to cook, by myself, with my kids or even with the grandchildren. How fortunate I was cooking became part of my life. All I needed to do was read a cook book; the rest was up to me. Being a mother to all those children, trying to teach them right from wrong, how to be fair, honest, loving and kind, that was not easy. I had to learn to become a good mother, not from books but from experience. I tried to raise them all the same but they did not all respond the same. No two are alike. Sometimes I wonder if they learned more from me or if I learned more from them. It's a toss up. It is much easier to be a good Grandma or great grandma, just love them.

I have been given a gift from God and I want to share it with everyone. The richest person on this earth does not have what I have. It is worth more than silver and gold. This treasure I have is an abundance of love. Where is the source of this never ending love? My main supply of love comes from God of course. My secondary supply comes from something he gave me, children. I had eight children of my own, inherited two very wonderful sons from my first husband, two loving daughters from my last husband and the supply just keeps on coming. My Pastor, we call him Pastor Stace, is also just like a son to me and his wife and children are considered my family as well. All of my children got married and their husbands and wives have become my children. All of my children had children of their own, then their children had children and it just keeps going. The best part is they all belong to me.

My family is growing so fast it is mind boggling. But let me tell you, after growing up as a child in a house full of children and then spending the better part of my adult life with a home full of children, it is not easy growing old alone. I am very fortunate that there is always one of them calling or visiting me. I also have the privilege of talking to many of them on a daily basis on Facebook. I love listening to each on tell me about the places they are going, meeting all their friends and learning about all the things they are doing each day. They share their joys, their plans for their future and often divulge troubles in more detail then they realize. It's a new age for me. What a wonderful thing Facebook is. I get to hear and see how they are all doing in their life from all over the United States. I have family in Washington, New Mexico, Texas, Kansas, Atlanta, Omaha, Nebraska, Council Bluffs, Iowa, Denver, Colorado, the Carolinas, the Dakotas, Nixa, Missouri, Idaho, Arizona, and New York and all over California and Oregon. There is no way I could keep up with all of them without Facebook. The joy I have just opening up Facebook and there they are, talking to me. I so much enjoy viewing all the pictures and remotely watching all of them grow. I truly love the life I am living. If I was alone, without all my family, my life would be boring, a word I try hard never to use. I am so happy I am not an old lady just getting up each morning and doing the same thing. Even at my age I am happy to say that this old lady has a future. This constant barrage of information stimulates my brain and gives me plenty to think about besides myself. Our brain is the most important part of our body. Depending on how you use it, it can make you happy or sad. It's fascinating to know that we actually have a built-in sense to guide our brains in whatever direction we choose. It's basically your conscience. Pay attention to it. Depending on the information we take in we can lead it in the right or the wrong direction. I try real hard to keep my mind healthy and happy. I don't dwell on how old I am but how wise I have become. Like my Grandma said, "It's not how long you live it's how well you live." God has blessed me with all these children. When I take the initiative to watch and listen to what they are saying and doing, it keeps me not only young at heart but young in mind. Everything else in my life is icing on the cake. I love you all.